A Practical Guide to Counseling Veterans

Kristi Kanel

California State University, Fullerton

CENGAGE
Learning

Australia • Brazil • Mexico • Singapore • United Kingdom • United States

For product information and technology assistance, contact us at **Cengage Learning Customer & Sales Support, 1-800-354-9706**.

For permission to use material from this text or product, submit all requests online at **www.cengage.com/permissions** Further permissions questions can be emailed to **permissionrequest@cengage.com**.

Cover Image: ©Klemin Misic/Shutterstock

ISBN: 978-1-305-40101-3

Cengage Learning
20 Channel Center Street
Boston, MA 02210
USA

Cengage Learning is a leading provider of customized learning solutions with office locations around the globe, including Singapore, the United Kingdom, Australia, Mexico, Brazil, and Japan. Locate your local office at: **www.cengage.com/global**.

Cengage Learning products are represented in Canada by Nelson Education, Ltd.

To learn more about Cengage Learning Solutions, visit **www.cengage.com**.

Purchase any of our products at your local college store or at our preferred online store **www.cengagebrain.com**.

Printed in the United States of America
Print Number: 01   Print Year: 2014

Contents

Introduction

Since the terrorist attacks on the World Trade Center and the Pentagon on 9/11/2001 (9/11), and when Iraq was invaded due to the fear that they possessed weapons of mass destruction, the United States has been involved in two major wars, **Operation Iraqi Freedom (OIF) and Operation Enduring Freedom (OEF).** Over a million men and women have served their country in these two wars and are now returning home. Many of these service personnel bring back with them wounds. Some wounds are physical such as amputated legs; others are invisible such as posttraumatic stress disorder (**PTSD**), depression, and **traumatic brain injury (TBI).** It is these *invisible wounds* that counselors are likely to work with in a variety of settings. Although less military personnel have died in recent wars than in past wars, many are returning with emotional and psychological scars and need help healing them. Also, many women have participated in these wars, which has led to an increase in military sexual assaults.

Key Concepts

Antiadrenergics: These medications are sometimes used for the treatment of hyperarousal, irritable aggression, intrusive memories, nightmares, and insomnia for those with chronic PTSD.

Battle fatigue: This was what the veterans of WW I were said to be suffering from when they showed symptoms of what we now call PTSD.

Benzodiazepines: This is a class of medication sometimes used to reduce extreme arousal and anxiety and to improve sleep.

Cognitive Restructuring: This type of therapy focuses on helping the client identify irrational, unrealistic beliefs and change them to more realistic ways of viewing the situation.

Combat stress injuries: This is a phrase that refers to various psychological challenges that veterans experience due to military service such as depression, posttraumatic stress disorder, and traumatic brain injury.

Department of Defense (DOD): This is the umbrella federal agency that houses the Veterans Health Administration (VHA) and Department of Veteran Affairs (VA) as well as the central command post for the armed services of the United States.

Deployment: When a military service member is called to go to a base throughout the world and serve either in combat or in a support role.

Eye Movement Desensitization and Reprocessing (EMDR): This is a type of exposure therapy in which the client works through the emotions and thoughts involved in a traumatic event.

Exposure Therapy: This type of therapy involves having the client visualize or view stimuli that replicates a traumatic event. Emotional and cognitive components are also discussed during the exposure.

Hypervigilance: This is a common symptom of PTSD in which the person is extremely alert and on edge about danger occurring.

Invisible wounds: These are common in OIF and OEF veterans. Whereas in previous wars, most veterans returned with physical wounds, these new veterans are returning with high prevalence of PTSD, depression and TBI which aren't also visible to the average person.

Military Sexual Trauma (MST): When someone has been sexually harassed or assaulted while serving in the military.

Operation Enduring Freedom (OEF): The name given to the war in Afghanistan that began after the attacks on 9/11.

Operation Iraqi Freedom (OIF): The name given to the war fought in Iraq that began in 2003.

OxyContin: A pain-killer often prescribed to war veterans. It is also used as an illicit drug.

Pharmacotherapy: This refers to the use of medication in treating anxiety, flashbacks and sleep disorders.

Post-deployment: When a veteran returns home from active service.

Posttraumatic Stress Disorder (PTSD): This is a syndrome that occurs sometimes after someone experiences a life threatening trauma and includes many symptoms such as numbing, anxiety, depression, flashbacks, sleep disorders, and hypervigilance.

Pre-deployment: This is the phase of deployment that occurs when the service member has just been told s/he will be traveling to go serve in combat.

Secondary traumatization: This often occurs when loved ones are around a veteran who is suffering from PTSD. The loved one begins to experience certain symptoms of PTSD themselves.

Shell shock: This term was used to describe symptoms often seen in WWII veterans when they returned from combat. It is very similar to PTSD.

Traumatic Brain Injury (TBI): This is a signature wound of OIF and OEF veterans. It occurs when exposed to firefights, IEDs, and other bombs. Symptoms include loss of memory, poor concentration, and other neurological disorders.

Trauma and Stressor-Related Disorder: This is the classification that PTSD now belongs to in the Diagnostic and Statistical Manual of Mental Disorders 5th edition. PTSD was formerly classified as an anxiety disorder.

Veterans Affairs(VA): This is a branch of the DOD that concerns itself with the many regulations, rights, benefits and needs of veterans.

Veterans Health Administration (VHA): This is the branch of the DOD that focuses on the medical needs of veterans.

Virtual Reality Exposure: This type of exposure therapy uses computer programs to help veterans re-experience the scenarios in Iraq and Afghanistan that simulate their trauma.

An Historical View of Serving in the Military and PTSD

Professional focus on the psychological and emotional issues facing veterans became heightened after the Vietnam War. Prior to that war, psychologists were aware that veterans were affected by military service, but had no language to discuss the particulars of the suffering. In 1980, the American Psychiatric Association added the syndrome Posttraumatic Stress Disorder to its diagnostic nomenclature. The Vietnam War drawdown was complete by then, and counselors and social workers were given the duty to work with the many veterans who had returned suffering from PTSD. Unfortunately, at that time, the primary service provided was assessment for disability rather than cure. Vietnam veterans' symptoms have included re-experiencing the sounds of war, suffering from nightmares, and being unable to manage interpersonal relationships effectively. Support groups were set up to allow these veterans an opportunity to discuss their traumas and to find ways to integrate their war experiences into present-day functioning.

The veterans of World War II had similar responses to their combat experiences. Anyone who exhibited signs of trauma was said to have **shell shock**. Unfortunately, many World War II veterans did not seek or receive mental health treatment when they returned home in the same way that veterans of the Vietnam War and veterans of more recent wars have done. They were encouraged to "buck up" and "be a man." While it is true that veterans of the Iraq and Afghanistan wars have also been told to be strong and deal with "it" on their own, many have rejected these ideas and have sought treatment despite being told they don't really need it. Films such as *Saving Private Ryan* have put a realistic perspective on the extent of the trauma experienced by the men serving in World War II. It is easy to forget that they suffered because, unlike their Vietnam veteran counterparts, World War II veterans received a hero's welcome when they returned home. World War II was a popular war, and most Americans were supportive of the efforts of the military.

The veterans of World War I were said to suffer from **Battle Fatigue.** It seems that the phenomenon we now call PTSD is a result of the introduction of gun fire into the battle situation. When battle just included swords and people running at you, the soldier knew what was coming. Fire fights seem to induce more symptoms of **hypervigilance**, and recent studies have shown that soldiers who have engaged in firefights suffer from PTSD more than those who did not.

While soldiers are engaged in combat and see the trauma of war, some do experience acute stress disorder. They are often treated by doctors and given time to recuperate. However, the military does such a good job of training soldiers to numb themselves to war trauma that the majority are able to deal with combat as it is happening. It is when they return home that they show signs of PTSD. The disorder has been delayed, almost, by training. Once soldiers return home, many have difficulty adjusting to civilian life. They report being preoccupied with the troops that are still fighting. They often feel guilty for leaving the other soldiers and think they should return to help fight.

The recent wars fought in Iraq and the Persian Gulf have also left emotional scars on combat veterans. Some refer to the PTSD experienced by soldiers who fought to free Kuwait in the 1990s as Persian Gulf syndrome. As the soldiers began returning home after deployments in the Iraq and Afghanistan wars, their psychological and emotional reactions have been studied by clinicians treating them in clinics and by other interested social scientists. It has been shown that they too show symptoms of PTSD, acute stress disorder and depression upon their return and while engaged in combat (Kanel, 2015).

OIF and OEF Veterans

Those serving in OIF were stationed in Iraq or provided support to those military personnel. Those serving in OEF were stationed in Afghanistan or supported those serving in Afghanistan. There are many unique aspects to how these veterans have been treated by mental health professionals at the **Veteran's Health Administration (VHA)** and by their combat units compared to veterans of other wars. For example, in 2009, the army was giving 225,000 soldiers some form of behavioral health care and almost half of them were on mood-stabilizing prescription drugs. Ten percent had been prescribed narcotic painkillers like **OxyContin**, leading to widespread abuse (Philipps, 2010).

Statistics

Over 2.4 million service members have been deployed to Afghanistan or Iraq since October 2001 (VHA Office of Public Health, 2010).

Approximately 15–20% of combat troops have symptoms of anxiety or depression (MHAT, 2008; Miliken, Auchterlonie & Hoge, 2007 and Tanielian & Jaycox, 2008). Disorder Risk increases to 35.5% at six months post-deployment (Miliken, et al., 2007).

Military Culture

It is not a stretch to imagine that the armed forces indoctrinate military personnel to believe that mental health problems are a source of weakness. This may cause the service member to perceive counseling for emotional issues as weak. Honor, courage, loyalty, integrity, and commitment are highly valued in the military which leads to high ethical standards but may hamper mental health utilization (Coll, Weiss, & Metal, 2013). A warrior mentality is also promoted. Counselors would be well advised to utilize this concept, and instead of encouraging the soldier to give up the warrior mentality, the counselor can help the veteran dial up or down the warrior response depending on the situation.

Counselors must keep in mind this military culture when treating veterans. They must also be aware that many of the veterans engaged in killing enemy combatants and civilians. Some of the returning veterans who seek treatment may have experienced the stages of killing another human being. Counselors may wish to provide education and understanding of their experience. Grossman (1995) describes the five stages of killing as including concern, killing, exhalation, remorse and finally rationalization and acceptance. By educating the veteran about the normalcy of going through these stages, it might provide some relief and normalization.

There has however been a major effort to destigmatize mental health concerns, including the development and implementation of preventative programs providing short-term, immediate counseling for service members and family, which are being well received and highly utilized. These services will be discussed in more detail below.

The military expects that soldiers will experience combat stress reactions. Even those not directly exposed to combat are taxed physically and emotionally in ways they are not prepared for, despite training and preparation. The pure physical demands of war-zone activities affect the stress hormones which sustain the body's alarm reaction. This helps soldier retain their fighting edge. Alertness and hypervigilance have survival value in battle. Unfortunately these same reactions do not work adaptively in the civilian world and are a big component of PTSD sufferers.

Counselors can help veterans feel less shame and stigma by reframing their stress reactions as an occupational hazard. These emotional symptoms are even more frequently seen than physical injury in these most recent wars. The veteran suffering from PTSD or depression deserves the same amount of respect and dignity as the veteran who lost a limb. By referring to emotional disorders as **combat stress injuries,** the veteran might be helped to destigmatize their experience and may be more likely to seek help. According to Shay (2009), injury is more culturally acceptable than a mental disorder.

Combat Fatigue Casualties

A very small percentage of soldiers become what are known as *combat fatigue casualties*, that is, they cease to function militarily as a combatant and act in a manner that endangers himself or herself and fellow soldiers. This soldier would be evacuated from the battle area. The features of severe incapacitating war-zone stress reactions are: restlessness, psychomotor deficiencies, withdrawal, increased sympathetic nervous system activity (symptoms related to anxiety such as increased heart palpitations, sweating, or increased pulse), stuttering, confusion, nausea, vomiting, and severe suspiciousness and distrust. Mental health counselors should keep in mind that most combatants are young and that during the late teens and early 20s, a person is at greatest risk for psychological decompensation, especially when that person has a history of family psychopathology. Just a small number of veterans are diagnosed with stress-induced mental illness (Brohl and Ledford, 2012, p.98-99). These differ from the disorders to be discussed below.

War-Zone Stressors (Brohl & Ledford, p. 100)

Lack of Preparation: Many veterans report being angry about not perceiving themselves as being sufficiently prepared or trained for what they experienced in the war. Perhaps they didn't believe they had the right equipment and supplies or lacked training on how to perform procedures and tasks. Maybe they didn't feel prepared for what their role would be. This lack of preparedness may lead to increased feelings of helplessness and unpredictability, factors that have been shown to increase risk for PTSD.

Combat Exposure: OIF and OEF veterans have probably been exposed to warfare experiences such as firing a weapon, being fired on, witnessing injury and death, and going on special missions and patrols that involve such experiences. Clinicians should be careful not to minimize any combat exposure, as even one experience could lead to PTSD.

Aftermath of battle: In addition to combat exposure, current veterans may also have been exposed to the consequences of combat such as observing or handling the remains of civilians, enemy soldiers, U.S. and allied personnel, or animals. They may have also observed devastated communities and homeless refugees or been involved in removing dead bodies after battle. Even exposure to the sight, sound, or smell of dying men and women may be intensely demoralizing and disturbing.

Perceived threat: Veterans may also report acute terror and panic and sustained anticipatory anxiety about potential exposure to circumstances of combat, including nuclear weapons, biological or chemical agents, missiles and friendly fire incidents. Research has shown that perceptions of life-threat are powerful predictors of post-war mental health outcomes.

Difficult living and working environment: While these may be lower level stressors, they are circumstances that are experienced daily. Personal discomforts or deprivations may be irritating and lead to feelings of pressure and may tax available coping resources. The need to learn to accommodate lack of desirable food, lack of privacy, poor living arrangements, uncomfortable climate, boredom, inadequate equipment and long workdays are typical low level stressors.

Concerns about life and family disruptions: Some troops may worry about how their deployment might negatively affect other important life-domains such as careers, losing a job, missing out on a promotion, damaging family relationships, missing special events.

Sexual or gender harassment: Unfortunately, there have been many reports of sexual related assaults from troops serving in OIF and OEF. Military Sexual Trauma will be discussed below. In general, exposure to any harassment may cause stress whether it be based on gender, minority status or social status. In addition to sexual misconduct, other forms of harassment include indirect resistance to authority, deliberate sabotage, indirect threats, constant scrutiny and gossip and rumors. These types of experiences create feelings of helplessness, powerlessness, rage and stress.

Ethno-cultural stressors: Soldiers from various minority ethnic groups may experience racism and discrimination. Soldiers who appear to be of Arab background may be particularly subject to racial prejudice/stigmatization because of their similarity to the enemy. They may also experience conflict between their American identity and their identity related to their heritage. They may have encountered pejorative statements about Arabs and Islam and have heard soldier devalue the significance of loss of life among the enemy because they practice Islam. In fact, not all Arabs are Muslim, but unfortunately, some assume this and therefore experience these feelings of fear and anger toward them for the behaviors of Arab, Muslim extremists. There may also exist prejudice against gays, Latinos, African Americans and Asian Americans from other ethnic groups. While this type of prejudice exists in everyday civilian life, when it occurs in the military it may be especially hurtful because soldier work side by side and need to trust that other soldiers have their back.

Counselors must consider that any of these stressors might be a component of PTSD, depression, suicidal thoughts, or alcohol and substance abuse for which a veteran might seek help. Since research shows that cognitive processing therapy is useful in reducing symptoms of PTSD, it is vital for counselors to guide PTSD sufferers into exploring any beliefs they have about any of these stressors.

Invisible Wounds

The veterans returning from OIF and OEF have been particularly vulnerable to experiencing what are called **invisible wounds.** These were discussed above as combat stress reactions or occupational hazards. Several of these types of wounds will be discussed below. Of course, veterans will seek services from mental health professionals for help with invisible wounds because physicians deal with the physical wounds. This discussion is not meant to discount the traumatic experiences of those veterans who have suffered physical wounds. In fact, there is growing evidence that physical injury during **deployment** is associated with a higher prevalence of mental health issues **post-deployment.** Many of these physically injured soldiers will experience PTSD and TBI. Taber & Hurley (2009) note a recent survey of soldiers following their return from deployment with findings showing that 9% of military personnel who had not been injured while deployed screened positive for PTSD while that rate was doubled, 16%, in those reporting bodily injury during deployment. However, as counselors, our purpose is to help with the PTSD and TBI, not repair physical injury. We must keep in mind that physical injury is an additional stressor for someone who may have experienced PTSD even without being physically injured. Please refer to the chapter entitled "A Practical Guide to PTSD" for a detailed discussion of the causes, the symptoms and interventions for PTSD in general. This discussion focuses exclusively on the PTSD suffered by veterans.

Posttraumatic Stress Disorder (PTSD)

As of 2011, in the military, the PTSD diagnosis no longer requires a specific experience of a specific event with verifiable time and date. The ongoing exposure to war itself can justify the diagnosis (Department of Veteran Affairs, 2012). The PTSD rates for veterans of OIF and OEF are thought to be 12.5% (Hoge, et al., 2004). Some studies show that two or more deployments could raise the rates of PTSD (Yarvis & Schiess, 2008). In a study conducted by Kanel in 2007 (2014), 21% of enrolled college student veterans qualified for a diagnosis of PTSD and 49% met the criteria for ASD while in the war zone.

Following is a list of the formal symptoms and criteria listed in the Diagnostic and Statistical Manual of Mental Disorders -5th Edition (DSM-5) for a diagnosis of PTSD according to the American Psychiatric Association (2013). This diagnosis is no longer considered an anxiety disorder but instead it is now considered a **trauma and stressor-related disorder.**

    A. **Stressor:** A person must have been exposed to death, threatened death, actual or threatened serious injury, or actual or threatened sexual violence either by:
   1) direct exposure
   2) witnessing in person
   3) indirectly by learning that a close relative or close friend was exposed to trauma as long as the actual or threatened death involved was violent or accidental

    B. **Intrusion symptoms:** The traumatic event must be persistently re-experienced in at least one of the following ways:
   1) recurrent, involuntary and intrusive memories (children older than 6 may express this in repetitive play)
   2) traumatic nightmares (children may have frightening dreams without content related to the trauma)
   3) dissociative reactions (e.g. flashbacks) which may occur on a continuum from brief episodes to complete loss of consciousness (children may reenact the event in play)
   4) intense or prolonged distress after exposure to traumatic reminders
   5) marked physiologic reactivity after exposure to trauma-related stimuli

C. **Avoidance:** The person experiences at least one persistent effortful avoidance of distressing trauma-related stimuli after the event such as:

   1) trauma-related thoughts of feelings

   2) trauma-related external reminders (e.g. people, places, conversations, activities, objects, or situations)

D. **Negative alterations in cognitions and mood**: The person experiences at least two of the following symptoms that are indicative of negative alterations in cognitions and mood that began or worsened after the traumatic event:

   1) inability to recall key features of the traumatic event (usually dissociative amnesia, not due to head injury, alcohol, or drugs)

   2) persistent (and often distorted) negative beliefs and expectations about oneself or the world (e.g., "I am bad." "the world is completely dangerous.")

   3) persistent distorted blame of self or others for causing the traumatic event or for resulting consequences

   4) persistent negative trauma-related emotions (e.g., fear, horror, anger, guilt, or shame)

   5) markedly diminished interest in (pre-traumatic) significant activities

   6) feeling alienated from others (e.g., detachment or estrangement)

   7) constricted affect: persistent inability to experience positive emotions

E. **Alterations in arousal and reactivity:** The person experiences at least two of the following trauma-related alterations in arousal and reactivity that began or worsened after the traumatic event:

   1) irritable or aggressive behavior

   2) self-destructive or reckless behavior

   3) hypervigilance

   4) exaggerated startle response

   5) problems in concentration

   6) sleep disturbance

F. **Duration:** The symptoms in the above criteria 2, 3, 4, and 5 must have existed for more than one month.

G. Functional significance: The person experiences significant symptom-related distress or functional impairment socially, occupationally, academically, behaviorally, and so on.

H. Exclusion: The disturbance is not due to medication, substance use, or other illness.

Additionally, the person experiences high levels of one of the following dissociative symptoms:

1. **Depersonalization:** The person experiences him or herself as being an outside observer of or detached from oneself (e.g., feeling as if "this is not happening to me" or one were in a dream).
2. **Derealization:** The person experiences life as not real, from a distance or with distortions (e.g. "things are not real").

Lastly, the diagnosing clinician must specify if the PTSD is with **delayed expression** where a full diagnosis is not met until at least six months after the trauma.

Anger and PTSD

Jakupcak et al. (2007) found that symptoms of PTSD have been found to be associated with anger, hostility, and aggression among OIF and OEF veterans. Teten et al. (2010) found that impulsive aggression was overrepresented among veterans with PTSD whereas premeditated aggression was found more in veterans without PTSD. Some of the risk factors related to aggression in veterans are having a background involving violence and aggression, firing weapons in combat, and long deployments (Elbogen et al., 2010).

Alcohol Misuse and PTSD

PTSD has also been found to be associated with high rates of alcohol abuse. Alcohol misuse often leads to a decrease in overall functional health which helps us understand that veterans suffering from PTSD who are not functioning well in terms of health, may also be misusing alcohol (McDevitt-Murphy et al., 2010). This relationship is important to keep in mind as many veterans may seek help for physical problems since the stigma attached to poor physical health isn't as severe as it is for mental health problems and for alcohol related problems. Since it is known that alcohol and substance abuse are related to physical health, it is vital that counselors guide veterans into proper treatment even when they seek medical help only. Since mental health services carry a stronger negative stigma than physical health services, counselors might reframe the need for specific substance abuse treatment as being necessary for physical health rather than suggesting it is a mental health disorder (Kanel, 2014, p. 181).

Alcohol misuse has also been found to be a precipitating factor for suicidality and aggression (Jakupcak et al., 2007; Lemaire & Graham, 2011; Taft, Street, Marshall, Dowdall, & Riggs, 2007), which makes it even more essential for counselors to be aware of tendencies for alcohol misuse among this population, tuning into the relationship between alcohol misuse, depression, anger, and self-destructive behaviors (Kanel, 2014, p. 181).

Military Sexual Trauma (MST) and PTSD

As mentioned previously, sexual harassment may be a stressor that induces PTSD in military personnel. Military sexual trauma (MST) is a unique situation due to the sociopolitical aspects of the relationship between the victim and perpetrator. **MST** can be defined as sexual violence occurring while serving in the military and occurs in both men and women, but the prevalence is much higher in women. The issues facing victims/survivors of military sexual assault in many ways are similar to acquaintance rape because the victim almost always knows the perpetrator. However, there are many special considerations to keep in mind when working with victims of sexual assault that took place while serving in the military. Many women describe horrific sexual assault experiences such as being drugged and raped during basic training, to being fired for being raped. Others who report being sexually assaulted in the military are diagnosed with a personality disorder for failing to adjust adequately to being raped.

One of the unique aspects of the OIF and OEF wars was the fact that women veterans made up nearly 10% of total veteran user population at the **VHA** by the year 2010. As of 2005, women occupied more than 80% of all military occupational specialties and 90% of careers in the military (Pierce, 2006). As of 2010 women comprised 15% of the total active force and it was expected that this figure would increase (Moore & Kennedy, 2011). Schading (2007) points out that one of the reasons for not allowing women to serve historically in active fighting is because

13

of the possibility of romance and rape inherent because they are weaker. Unfortunately, because the military has not had a zero tolerance of inappropriate sexual behavior, some of this is a reality. Not necessarily because the woman is physically weaker, but because the rapist is in a position of power. Not only do women have to struggle with stereotypes if they serve in the military, they also must deal with isolation and few role models and mentors (Moore & Kennedy, 2001).

Women often do not report MST due to fears of revenge, scorn and negative work repercussions (Pierce, 2006). Katz et al., (2007) found that in their sample of 18 women who had served in OIF/OEF that 56% reported Military Sexual Assault. All 10 of these assaulted women were sexually harassed (experiencing sexually inappropriate, degrading, or suggestive comments), 6 of the 10 reported unwanted physical advances, and 3 of the 10 reported being raped. They also found that the women who experienced MST reported significantly greater difficulties with readjustment and were rated by clinicians as having more severe symptoms compared to those who were not sexual traumatized. These women are at higher risk for developing PTSD than those who were physically injured or who witnessed others being injured. Of course, men who are sexually assaulted while serving in the military will also suffer from PTSD, and they are probably less likely to report it than women. Because of this lack of reporting, statistics regarding MST and men is probably not accurate. Common sense tells us though that if PTSD is more likely in women who suffer MST, it will be higher in men as well.

Depression and Suicide

Kanel's study of college-enrolled veterans surveyed symptoms of major depression in this group (2014). The symptoms of major depression include sleep problems, feelings of guilt, worthlessness, hopelessness, regret, loss of energy and interest in life, concentration deficits, appetite disorder, psychomotor retardation, agitation, and suicidal thoughts. The symptoms of depression most frequently reported were, "depressed mood most of the day, fatigue or loss of energy nearly every day, and insomnia or hypersomnia" with 50 %, 45%, and 50% reporting these symptoms, respectively. To meet the DSM criteria for Major Depression, at least five symptoms must be reported(APA, 1994). Twenty-seven percent of respondents answered "yes" to at least five, indicating that the rate of major depression among college enrolled veterans is about 27%, higher than that for PTSD. Keep in mind however, that now that

PTSD is considered a stress reaction disorder rather than an anxiety disorder, it may be that some veterans manifest their PTSD via depression symptoms more than through typical PTSD symptoms. Most clinicians and researches will agree that depression is highly associated with the PTSD experienced by the OIF and OEF veterans.

According to the National Survey on Drug Use and Health, (2008), approximately 9.3% of veterans experienced at least one major depressive episode in 2007, leading to impairment in functioning. Kanel's survey took place in 2007 as well, but the results of her survey show almost triple the national rate. Perhaps college-enrolled veterans are at higher risk of depression because many are single. Her study showed a significant correlation between being single and having more symptoms of depression. Another guess would be that college-enrolled veterans are in flux regarding a career, and college creates stress that those already in the workforce don't face. Also, college-enrolled veterans must interact with young college students who often don't have the same work ethic and discipline as veterans. This may cause feelings of alienation and social withdrawal.

Suicide among veterans: Suicide is a symptom of depression, and in the veterans of OIF and OEF suicide is not uncommon. In 2007, the Veterans Crisis Line answered more than half a million calls and made more than 18,000 life-saving rescues. In 2009, this crisis line helped more than 28,000 people (Department of Veterans Affairs, 2011).The Veterans Crisis Line received more than 890,000 calls between October 2006 and June 2013. As of 2007, veterans completed suicide at a rate far exceeding the nonveteran population (Hampton, 2007). There were 108 confirmed suicides completed among young enlisted unmarried while males, who used firearms as their means (U.S. Department of Defense Task Force on Mental Health, 2007).

Drugs and/or alcohol were involved in 30% of the suicide cases in 2007 (U.S. Army Suicide Event Report). Many of those suicides and attempts were preceded by a failed intimate relationship. The study found a significant relationship between suicide and number of days deployed to Iraq or Afghanistan. Also, many of the soldiers who were medically evacuated for psychiatric problems were also found to have engaged in self-harm behavior.

Suicide among veterans is on the increase. More soldiers are dying from suicide than were killed in combat (Tarabay, 2010). In 2009, 245 military personnel died of suicide and as of May 2010, there were already 163 suicides completed. In a study that surveyed 21 states from 1999 to 2011, it was reported that 22 veterans commit suicide every day; (Department of Veterans Affairs 2013). The Veterans Crisis Line received more than 890,000 calls between October 2006 and June 2013.

It is possible that the reason so many veterans are attempting and completing suicide is because very few of them seek mental health treatment despite suffering from PTSD and depression. When someone suffers from these types of combat stress injuries, and doesn't seek help, sometimes the pain is so intense that the person perceives suicide as the only way out of the pain.

Hoge, et al. (2004) found that out of the 731 soldiers and marines who screened positively for a mental health problem:

- 65% said that they would be considered weak if they sought help.
- 63% indicated that were concerned that their unit leadership would treat them differently if they sought help.
- 59% stated that members of their unit might have less confidence in them if they sought help.
- 55% indicated that it would be difficult to get time off of work for treatment.
- 50% were concerned that if they sought help it would hurt their career.
- 45% reported that it was difficult to schedule an appointment for help.
- 41% reported that if they sought help it would be too embarrassing.
- 38% indicated that they did not trust mental health professionals and so did not seek help.
- 25% indicated that mental health care doesn't work and costs too much so they didn't seek help.
- 18% reported that they didn't have adequate transportation to get help.

One of the ways to reduce suicide would be to reduce the stigma associated with seeking assistance for mental health care by making it clear to all military personnel that just as physical injuries are expected in combat, so are mental health issues. If the veteran would seek help as soon as s/he began to experience the mental health injury, treatment would have a better chance of preventing suicide and other serious impairments in functioning. After a report by the National Public Radio in 2006 (Zwerdling, 2009), it was discovered that soldiers requesting mental health assistance from providers at Fort Carson, Colorado were told that there was nothing wrong with them, dismissed some as cowards, and discharged some from the service. Investigations were conducted by the Senate, the Government Accountability Office and the Pentagon and in an effort to reduce stigma for seeking mental health care, the Army started a program at Fort Bragg, North Carolina in which they moved the behavioral (mental) health personnel into medical facilities (Kerr, 2007 cited in Pryce et al, 2012, p. 75). A Department of Defense task force has recommended that outreach to the troops, including screening and prevention, may get them into clinics more quickly. However, the military health system is overloaded and has insufficiently qualified providers to promptly reach everyone concerned. Some officers in charge of military health at the highest levels still continue to believe that there is no direct correlation between war and suicide (Kerr, 2007 cited in Pryce et al., 2012, p. 75).

But suicide among veterans did not go away. Shortly after this task force made their recommendation, Congress passed the Joshua Omvig Veterans Suicide Prevention Act into law on November 6, 2007. This was precipitated by one veteran's suicide after completing an eleven month tour in Iraq. Upon his return home, he began having symptoms of PTSD and shared his concerns with his family. They encouraged him to seek help, but he did not, fearing it would have a negative effect on his military career. He told his mother that he felt dead inside and later shot himself in front of his mother (Jacobs, 2006; Magee, 2006 cited in Pryce et al., 2012, p. 76). This Act requires the Veterans Health Administration (VHA) to develop a suicide prevention program to address the growing number of veterans who complete suicide. It requires that all veteran's affairs staff receive mental health training, that every VHA medical center have a suicide counselor, that veterans receiving care at a VHA facility will have mental health screening and receive treatment when appropriate and at the veteran's request, and that veterans have 24-hour access to the VHA for mental health care and an available VHA suicide hotline.

Guerra and Calhoun (2010) found that the risk of suicide was uniquely associated with PTSD among 393 veterans they studied. The strongest relationship found was between numbing (detachment and limited affect) and suicidality. They also found that the cognitive-affective dimension of depressive symptoms was highly correlated with suicidality. So while depression does predict suicidal thoughts, PTSD does as well so counselors should always assess suicidal thoughts when working with a veteran suffering from PTSD.

Another factor related to suicide by veterans has to do with killing. Selby et al. (2010) argued that the more experience a veteran had with killing, the greater is their acquired capability for suicide and their own death. Repeated exposure to killing in combat desensitizes soldiers in that it decreases the power of fear and pain and makes them less terrorizing.

Traumatic Brain Injury

Another frequent invisible wound that has come to the attention of physicians and counselors is traumatic brain injury (TBI). TBI remains the signature wound of OIF and OEF. Since 2000, it is estimated that more than 195,000 service members have been screened for a suspected brain injury (Department of Defense, 2009). Explosive munitions have caused 75% of all U.S. casualties resulting from the wars in Iraq and Afghanistan (Institute of Medicine, Committee on Gulf War and Health, 2008 cited in Pryce et al., 2012, p. 37). They describe the common causes of TBI as being exposed to improvised explosive devices (IEDs), car bombs, rocket-propelled grenades, mortars, and rockets. Being exposed to these military ammunitions affects one's neurological functioning in several ways. Symptoms of TBI may include decreased levels of consciousness, amnesia, poor concentration and other neurological irregularities (Tanielian & Jaycox, 2008). TBI may be mild, moderate or severe, depending on any period of loss of consciousness or decreased level of consciousness and any loss of memory for events immediately before or after the injury. For veterans enrolled in college or who are working a job that thinking, this can be challenging. It may cause impairments in thinking, judgment, attention span, concentration, memory, visuospatial skills, problem-solving skills and emotional stability.

Practice Considerations: Diversity, Ethics, Family, and College-enrolled Veterans

Ethnicity: Latinos, African Americans, Native Americans and Asians and Pacific Islanders have played an integral role in the U.S. military throughout history, having served as far back as the Revolutionary War and the Civil War. There have been challenges for these groups over the years such as an overrepresentation of Latinos and African Americans in the Vietnam War and segregation in WWII. Loyalties were sometimes questioned by undocumented immigrants serving and by Asians who wanted to serve in WWII. And no doubt some troops held racist beliefs as seen in civilian populations. Another aspect of minorities serving is the effect poverty has on someone being willing to serve as a way to earn a living. Those people coming from middle to upper income homes don't usually see the need to serve for money and are more likely to enlist as officers or seek employment elsewhere.

Sexual Orientation: Gays in the military is another diversity issue for counselors to keep in mind. There is no doubt that homosexuals have served in the military throughout history. In 1942, homosexuality was targeted as a means of screening out service members by the draft board. By 1993, President Clinton signed into law the "Don't Ask, Don't Tell, Don't Pursue" policy which prohibited the military from screening for homosexual behaviors. Once in, service members could not be asked if they were homosexual and anybody suspected of homosexuality could not be forced to reveal their orientation. This also meant that the person in question could not reveal him or herself as homosexual under punishment by dishonorable discharge which was deemed unfair by many. In 2010, "Don't Ask, Don't Tell" was repealed. This act took effect September 2011. It allows homosexual service personnel to live openly gay lifestyles just as heterosexual service personnel are permitted to live openly heterosexual lifestyles.

Aging: In 2010, 40% of veterans were 65 years or older. As they age, they hold different opinions about medical utilization; they are less likely than younger veterans to ask for medicine and are more likely to suffer in silence through pain due to arthritis and other natural ailments associated with aging (Appelt, Burant, Siminoff, Kwoh, &Ibrahim, 2007). Aging veterans may find that they have either late-onset PTSD or have been living with PTSD for many years pos-combat. Symptoms of PTSD may increase with age. According to the VHA (2012), there are four contributing factors to increased symptoms of PTSD: retirement, multiple medical problems, watching bad news and current conflicts on television, and a change in coping mechanisms such as not being able to drink alcohol due to a medical condition when the veteran had been using alcohol to cope for many years. PTSD can make it challenging for any veteran, no matter what age to address major stressors in life or live life to its fullest (VHA, 2012).

Gender: In addition to being the major victims of Military Sexual Trauma, women service members and veterans experience many other challenges not seen in their male counterparts. In particular, married military women must balance their workplace demands with their home environment. While civilian women tend to put their children first, military women must put the mission first. They must also plan how to keep the household running in their absence, something a husband/father doesn't usually feel responsible to do. Women in the military can be affected by all of the combat stress injuries discussed previously as well as having their spouse in the military, and due to these stresses married women in the military are three times more likely to get divorced than their male counterparts. Married military women are also more likely to be victims of domestic violence perpetrated by the civilian or military male spouse (Forgey & Badger, 2006). Unfortunately, female veterans are three times more likely than women civilians who never served in the military to complete suicide (Kennedy, 2010; McFarland, Kaplan & Huguet, 2010). The high rate of female veteran suicides was attributed to military-related sexual trauma as well as exposure to combat and injuries such as TBI. Another challenge for women in the military is managing their military obligations alongside of their menstrual cycle and pregnancies. There may limited access to restroom facilities and clean water or showers. This creates difficulties in hygiene, especially when the woman must travel for up to 8 hours before stopping sometimes (Trego, 2007). Pregnancy and childbirth raise other issues such as the ability to breastfeed, finding adequate child care, and the impact of separation on the mother-child bond (Weiss & DeBraber, 2013, p. 42).

Ethical Issues: There are various ethical dilemmas facing both uniformed and civilian counselors when caring for veterans. There are also differences when working with a uniformed military member compared to a veteran who is no longer with the military. At times, counselors work in agencies or have practices that are not military funded or involved. At other times, counselors work at locations funded by the Department of Defense (DOD); places like the VET Center patronize veterans as both visitors and counselors.

Counseling active military members: Ethical issues are much more complicated for those therapists working at a military base or working for the VHA because most of the clients are on active duty and the counselor must often communicate progress to military officials. Just as when a counselor receives a court-ordered referral or a work management referral, there can be confusion about exactly who the client is. In other words, where does the counselor's loyalty lie? At times, counselors make recommendations to employers and judges about the fitness of someone to return to work or to live in society. Counselors who work for the military often receive referrals and then must inform superior officers of a client's mental health and readiness for combat which creates challenges for the counselor, especially if that counselor is also an enlisted military service member. Regardless of where a therapist works, they must be guided by ethical standards. Most counselors have been trained to adhere to the ethical standards listed by various professional associations such as the American Psychological Association, the American Psychiatric Association, the National Association for Social Workers, the American Counseling Association, and the American Association for Marital and Family Therapists.

At times, the military may seek information or try to intervene in a service member's treatment which goes against the normal ethical process of a counselor. Social workers and counselors may find themselves play dual roles, feeling loyal to the military but also to the service member seeking counseling. Additionally, at times, the VHA may seek information from even civilian counselors to ascertain whether the veteran is eligible for continuing disability benefits. The counselor must provide information, but often feels like s/he is betraying the veteran.

In regards to confidentiality, counselors must accept that mission readiness and national security trumps all therapist-client privacy of confidentiality. Johnson et al. (2006, p. 314) provides nine recommendations for dealing with various ethical challenges:

1. Strive for a neutral posture in the community (of veterans). It can create the perception that you are available and nonpartisan.
2. Assume that every member of the community is a future client.
3. Provide immediate informed consent information to all clients.
4. Use stringent interpretations of 'need to know' policies and be conservative when determining what information is crucial to the question posed by a command.
5. Avoid significant self-disclosure.
6. Consider alternative mental health resources especially when complicated or awkward situations occur.
7. Increase tolerance for boundary crossings because the military community is small and multiple roles are inherent.
8. Actively collaborate with clients regarding management of nonclinical interactions. In this way you and the client both knowhow to respond to each other in informal contact.
9. Carefully document uncomfortable multiple relationships and your efforts to carefully document awareness of the problem, ethical reasoning, and clear efforts to resolve the dilemmas in the most expeditious fashion possible.

21

Another approach to understanding ethics has been presented by Loewenberg and Dolgoff (1992, p. 60) in their ranking of ethical principles as seen below:

Ethical Principles Screen (EPS)

1. Protection of life (in the military, this may be translated to mean protection of military mission, which is often on the same priority as protection of life); oftentimes when a mission fails, lives are lost and national security can be thwarted
2. Equality and inequality
3. Autonomy and freedom
4. Least harm
5. Quality of life
6. Privacy and confidentiality
7. Truthfulness and full disclosure

When providing mental health services to a military member on active duty, it may help a counselor to think about these ethical principles. Additionally, when working at a military location as a counselor, one may find conflicts between law and ethics. Johnson, Grasso, and Maslowski (2010, p. 551-552) recommend six ways to manage these conflicts:

1. Use negotiation skills and chain of command to reduce the tension and clarify the concern so any issue can be navigated legally and ethically.
2. Know your ethical code and relevant federal laws. Familiarize yourself with the Uniformed Code of Military Justice (http://www.ucmj.us/)
3. Develop a process for ethical decision making.
4. Recognize that military service does not overrule or negate one's identity and obligations as a health professional.
5. Seek to balance client's best interest with DOD regulations.
6. Work to reduce conflicts between ethical guidelines and federal law as an advocate.

Counseling veterans who are no longer active: In some ways when counseling veterans no longer active, ethical strategies are less complicated. The concern of being found out is not as strong; however, many veterans still have concerns about the military discovering their mental health issues. When counseling is completely voluntary and their disability benefits do not rely on their mental health status, counselors can proceed like any other client, following the guidelines of their profession. At other times, counselors may have to disclose certain information, as with anyone receiving disability. It's wise to inform the client of limits of confidentiality as you would any client. Veterans in particular need to be reassured that their previous commanding officer cannot be told of his or her counseling sessions.

In general, be prepared, knowledgeable and smart about navigating the military culture. Make sure you are clear as to the status of the client as an active member and any disability benefits s/he may be receiving.

Issues Facing Military Families

Families of veterans also feel the trauma of their loved ones serving in the military. It is not uncommon to think of the entire family as serving in the military, as everyone must sacrifice when one member serves. The issues facing military families differ, depending on which stage of deployment the service member is currently in when services are sought. Below is a brief review of the stages of deployment and some typical issues for military families:

1. **Pre-deployment**: When the service member is told that s/he will be deployed soon, it is common for that member to begin focusing on the mission and disconnecting from the family. The service member will go through rigorous training the unit's next combat encounter. Unit members are familiarized with the stressors they can expect to encounter in combat as well as stress reduction training (Pryce, Pryce, & Shackelford, 2012, p. 44). When the service member is notified of an impending deployment, family members have many reactions. It is natural to protest the loss of the service member and to feel despair and detachment. It is not unusual for couple to have arguments during this period (Pincus, et al., 2010 cited in Pryce, Pryce, & Shackelford, 2012, p. 135). The family may feel tension, anger, afraid, anxious and doubtful and may need help in learning strong coping skills during this phase. There have been psycho-educational programs developed to prepare military families of these types of feelings and how things in the family unit will change. These programs help the families anticipate ambiguous loss characterized by uncertainty, lack of clarity, vagueness, and indeterminacy (Boss, 1980, 1999, 2007 cited in Pryce et al., 2012, p. 135). Probably the greatest uncertainty is the idea that the service

member may be going into harm's way. Counselors working with families at this phase may remind them about the various ways to maintain contact with the service member such as email, texting, video cameras, phone calls and social networking websites.

2. **Deployment**: While the service member is away, family members have a range of experiences. They learn to function without the deployed service member. This may come as a shock, but eventually, the families learn to cope or not. It not, this could lead to maladaptive coping behaviors which may necessitate the intervention of a mental health provider. The spouse must take on the role as single parent in many instances and engage in behaviors that the service member would normally do. This can be confusing for the children at times. Once of the benefits to the children is increased resiliency and coping skills, especially when deployment involves moving regularly. They must learn to adapt to new school surroundings and establish friendships quickly. The parent left at home often seeks support from friends, family and other military families.

3. **Post-deployment**: When the service member returns, the family and the veteran often experience complex emotions. The service member must be reintegrated into the family and let go of "mission" mentality. The behaviors needed to serve are quite different from those used in family management and closeness. Not only role adjustments must be made, but the family must often learn to deal with the veteran's PTSD, depression, TBI, and anger issues that may have resulted from combat. It's not uncommon for children and spouses to experience **secondary traumatization** where they feel anxious, hypervigiliant, and distressed. It is important to realize that there are more children and spouses of veterans than actual veterans. The majority of the children are five years or older (Barker & Berry, 2009 cited in Pryce et al., 2012, p. 137). An estimated two million children have experienced the deployment of a parent and many have experienced the death of this parent. As of 2006, 1,600 children had lost a parent, with an unknown number of children having parents return home with serious injuries (Chartrand & Siegel, 2007 cited in Pryce et al., 2012, p. 137). These children and spouses need support from counselors to help them understand why they are also experiencing symptoms of PTSD and depression and how to take care of themselves and the veteran. The Department of Veterans Affairs (VA, U.S. Department of Veterans Affairs, 2011) has developed a program that provides support to family caregivers of OIF and OEF veterans with serious

injuries such as TBI, psychological trauma or other mental disorder as a result of military service. The VA has recognized the toll that caregiving may have on the caregivers. In general, counselors can support families by helping them claim their identity as a military family and help them focus on how they have mastered problems in the past. It is helpful to get the families to talk about their roles, rules and rituals and past family events so they can anchor themselves in who they are in the face of ambiguity. Counselors can remind the families that they too are serving their country which can create a sense of pride.

College-enrolled veterans: Lighthall, (2012, cited in Kanel, 2014, p. 183) offers ten principles for working with student veterans. Counselors should consider that the veterans are diverse, do not see themselves as victims, often feel alone on campus, may be unaware of their own mild TBI, don't like to hear things like "the wars were a waste of human life", etc. As with all veterans, counselors working with veterans in college might reframe combat trauma as an injury, not a mental illness. Veteran college students can be both excellent students due to discipline, seriousness, and pride, but may be hindered in their performance due to TBI and PTSD. Veteran centers at colleges can assist these veterans in feeling less alienated.

Key Techniques/Interventions

General Goals of Counseling Veterans

When beginning to establish a counseling relationship with a veteran, counselors would be well advised to learn from Vietnam veterans who suffered from serious PTSD and who didn't receive effective intervention upon their return. There are a few things that counselors will want to help prevent as much as possible: family breakdown, social withdrawal and isolation, employment problems, and alcohol and drug abuse (Brohl & Ledford, 2012). Other general considerations of care for veterans are to form a working alliance, connect veterans with each other, offer practical help with specific problems, and attend to the broad needs of the person. Brohl & Ledford, also offer an overview of various methods of treatment to help manage acute stress reactions and PTSD in veterans: education about post-traumatic stress reactions, training in coping skills, **exposure therapy**, **cognitive restructuring**, family counseling, residential rehabilitation treatment and **pharmacotherapy** to be offered by a physician (2012, p. 104-107). We now turn to a more detailed discussion of a few of these approaches.

Education about post-traumatic stress reactions: Educating veterans returning home from war is intended to improve understanding and recognition of symptoms, reduce fear and shame about symptoms, and normalize his or her experience. Education also provides the veteran with an understanding of how recovery is thought to take place and what types of treatment may be beneficial.

Training in coping skills: It may also be beneficial for veterans to be taught certain skills such as anxiety management (breathing retraining and deep relaxation, emotional grounding and anger management and communication). This type of training includes education, demonstration, rehearsal with feedback and coaching, repeated practice, and homework assignments.

Cognitive restructuring: This approach is designed to help the veteran identify and challenge distressing trauma-related beliefs. It focuses on educating the veteran about the relationship between thoughts and emotions, exploring common negative and irrational thoughts, and developing alternative ways of thinking.

Family counseling: This type of approach includes family education, couples counseling, family therapy, parenting classes, training in conflict resolution, and workshops. Since the primary source of support for the returning veteran is the family, involving the family in treatment is essential. Both the veteran and the family benefit from support to help with a smooth transition for both parties in the reintegration process.

Residential rehabilitation treatment: At times a veteran may need inpatient hospitalization when symptoms are severe. Family therapy, medication, individual therapy and group therapy are generally included in an inpatient model.

Pharmacotherapy: This refers to the use of medications prescribed by a physician, sometimes a psychiatrist, and at other times a general practitioner. Medications may include antidepressants, **benzodiazepines, or antiadrenergics.**

Prolonged Exposure Therapy: As previously discussed in the chapter on PTSD, cognitive-behavioral treatment with prolonged exposure appears to have the best-documented therapeutic efficacy when treating PTSD. Prolonged exposure is a program of exposure therapy based on Foa and Kozak's (1986) emotional processing theory which states that PTSD involves pathological fear structures that are activated when information represented in the structures is encountered. Successful treatment requires emotional processing of the fear structures to modify their pathological elements so that the stimuli no longer evoke fear. Imaginal exposure includes engaging mentally with the fear structure through repeatedly revisiting the traumatic event in a safe environment. The client with PTSD is guided and encouraged by the therapist to imagine, narrate, and emotionally process the traumatic event. The client is able to process the emotions relevant to the traumatic event and decondition the avoidance aspect of the PTSD. In general, exposure therapy can help correct faulty perceptions of danger, improve perceived self-control of memories and accompanying negative emotions and strengthen adaptive coping responses under conditions of distress (Brohl & Ledford, 2012, p. 105). There are several approaches that include exposure which will be presented next.

1. *Virtual Reality Exposure Therapy* using virtual Iraq/Afghanistan: In 2005, the University of Southern California (Rizzo, Reger, Gahm, Difede, & Rothbaum, 2009) began the development of a virtual Iraq scenario at the Institute for Creative Technologies (ICT). Subsequently a virtual Afghanistan scenario has also been created. These virtual scenarios consist of a series of virtual scenarios designed to represent relevant contexts for **Virtual Reality Exposure,** including Middle Eastern-theme city and desert road environments. In addition to the visual stimuli, directional 3D audio, vibrotactile and olfactory stimuli of relevance can be delivered. The presentation of additive, combat-relevant stimuli can be controlled by a therapist via separate "wizard of Oz" clinical interface, while in full audio contact with the client. It allows a clinician to customize the therapy experience to the particular needs of the client. The counselor can place the client in scenario locations that resemble the setting in which the traumatic events initially occurred and can gradually introduce and control real time "trigger" stimuli (visual, auditory, olfactory, and tactile) as is required to foster the anxiety modulation needed for therapeutic processing and habituation (Leaman, S., Rothbaum, B. O., Difede, J., Cukor, J., Gerardi, M., & Rizzo, A. (2013, p. 117). It is very much like the process developed in the 1970s by Joseph Wolpe in his systematic desensitization (Wolpe, J., 1973).

2. *Eye Movement Desensitization and Reprocessing (EMDR):* This approach was developed in the 1990s by Shapiro & Forrest (1997). There has been considerable success in helping a variety of individuals suffering from trauma-based disorders such as combat and sexual assault victims. EMDR targets all of the information related to the trauma, allowing the cognitive elements and emotional elements to be reprocessed. Part of the treatment includes facilitating the emotional adoption of positive self-beliefs such as "I am now in control" or "Now I have choices". Therapists who practice EMDR much become certified through specialized training.

3. *Sand Tray Therapy:* McCabe (cited in Kanel, 2014, p. 192) has been implementing Sand Tray Therapy with veterans for the past two years in her nonprofit agency, Nex4Vets in Irvine, CA. She describes this type of therapy as an expressive and projective mode of psychotherapy involving the unfolding and processing of intra- and interpersonal issues through the use of items as a nonverbal medium of communication. She has seen this model be successful for veterans who may be unable to express their trauma from combat verbally. The theory behind this model is that during trauma, the nervous system becomes dysregulated and the use of a sand tray with boundaries allows for the contained space to deal with the emotions which leads to regulation of the nervous system. Healing occurs as the client's disorganized nervous system finds regulation from the organization of the story pieces while in the presence of a therapist who is resonating with a calm and contained repose.

Intervention for MST

On October 5, 2005, the Sexual Assault Prevention and Response Office at the Department of Defense (DOD) created the first agency to monitor and report on sexual assault cases that take place in the military. The goal was to eliminate sexual assaults that take place in the military (Department of Defense, 2005). The DOD counted about 2,700 victims of sexual assault in 2011, but due to underreporting, it estimates that there were far more, maybe 19,000. The reporting of sexual assault has grown steadily since 2007, from 2,223 in 2007 to 2,723 in 2011 (Kitfield, 2012). Intervening with this population is still in the early stages since these women are just returning from service and have only begun to open up to mental health workers about their abuse. As with any sexually assaulted individual, a female veteran who has been sexually assaulted needs a sense of community support. Cognitive therapy will be useful in helping her change thoughts about the assault. Crisis counselors can help her reduce feelings of guilt, shame, and weakness by letting her know this behavior is unacceptable and was not her fault. She must understand that the perpetrator is the rapist and his motivation was to gain control over her and make her feel humiliated. She can reduce his control over her by holding her head up high, proving to herself she has done nothing wrong, Also, by talking with others, she can feel reassured that she was assaulted. She may need to learn about date and acquaintance rape to better understand what coercion and lack of consent really means. EMDR might also be useful. Counselors should also be aware of advocacy groups and current laws regarding military sexual assault and encourage her to utilize all of the services available.

Crisis workers must also keep in mind that she may also be suffering from P TSD due to war-related experiences and depression, suicidal thoughts, anger, and substance misuse in addition to MST. Intervention will include a multifaceted approach.

Summary

Working with veterans requires that counselors have a basic understanding of military culture as this indoctrination into the military affects whether a service member seeks treatment for mental health conditions and receives acceptance of a combat-related mental health condition. The signature wound for veterans of OIF and OEF is TBI, which causes memory and concentration problems, as well as depression and other emotional issues. The other invisible wounds, which could be referred to as combat-related injuries, are PTSD and depression. Sadly, OIF and OEF have completed and attempted suicide at very high rates, often because the stigma of admitting to a mental disorder inhibited them from getting the counseling they need. Another aspect of the OIF and OEF veterans is the increase in women serving compared to other wars. This has led to many issues including the increase in MST. Effective treatment of these veterans includes cognitive behavior therapy, prolonged exposure therapy, family therapy, and group therapy. There are many resources being developed to work with the veterans and their families sponsored by the Veterans Affairs agency, nonprofit agencies, and local social service agencies.

Further Resources

Veteran's Administration: There has been an increase in the utilization of military social workers both in uniform and those who work contractually on bases for the VA and other federal departments such as Homeland Security, as well as in community agencies. They engage in direct practice such as psychotherapy, case management, counseling, family psycho-education, and advocacy.

Vets Centers: Many of these centers look like homes in the community or a small office rather than a huge bureaucratic VA building. They employ veterans trained as mental health counselors as well as civilians interested in working with veterans. They offer individual, family, and group counseling.

Department of Social Services: These services focus on advocacy and rights of veterans. They ensure that veterans utilize the services to which they are entitled, including medical care, mental health care, and financial care.

Tragedy Assistance Program for Survivors: This program offers peer-based emotional support for survivors who have lost someone serving in the military. They provide grief and trauma resources and information to educate family and friends, as well as benefits information, workshops, and webinars. They also have a 24/7 crisis intervention service to connect family members who have experienced loss with a support person who quickly arrives at their home. Lastly, they offer regional military survivor grief camps for children.

Combat Paper Project: This program sponsors workshops in which veterans can use their combat uniforms to create cathartic works of art and can reconcile and share their personal experiences.

http://www.combatpaper.org

Military ONESOURCE: This is a free service provided by the Department of Defense to service members and their families to help with a broad range of concerns.

www.militaryonesource.mil.

The Wounded Warrior Project: This program serves military service members who incurred service-connected wounds, injuries, or illnesses on or after 9/11, and their families.

http://www.woundedwarriorproject.org/mission.aspx

Practice Activities

1. Locate and visit your local Vet Center and speak to counselors there.
2. Talk to 5 family members of a veteran. Identity some of their struggles and challenges.
3. Speak to a veteran and ask about what they are proud about and what some of their challenges have been.

References

American Psychiatric Association. (2013). *Diagnostic and statistical manual of mental disorder. (5th ed.)*. Washington, DC: Author.

American Psychiatric Association. (1994). *Diagnostic and statistical manual of mental disorder. (4th ed.)*. Washington, DC: Author.

Appelt, C. J., Burant, C. J., Siminoff, L.A., Kwoh, C. K, & Ibrahim, S. A. (2007). Arthritis-specific health beliefs related to aging among older male patients with knee and or hip osteoarthritis. *Journal of Gerontology, 62,* 2, 184-190.

Basu, M. (2013). Why suicide rate among veterans may be more than 22 a day. Retrieved 01/17/2014 http://www.cnn.com/2013/09/21/us/22-veteran-suicides-a-day/index.html

Brohl, K. & Ledford, R. (2012). The returning U.S. Veteran of Modern War: Background Issues, Assessment and Treatment. *Continuing Education for California Social Workers and Marriage and Family Therapists.* Phone: 1-866-653-2119 or www.elitecme.com

Coll, J. E., Weiss, E. L., & Metal, M. (2013). Military Culture and Diversity. Found in A. Rubin, E. L. Weiss, & J. E. Coll, (Eds). *Handbook of Military Social Work,* pages 21-36. New Jersey: John Wiley & Sons., Inc.

Department of Defense. (2009). Numbers for Traumatic Brain Injury. DVBIC.org

Department of Defense 6495.01. (2005). *Sexual assault prevention and response program.* Washington, D.C.

Department of Veterans Affairs. (2012). National Center for PTSD. How Cognitive Processing therapy can help. Retrieved 8/30/2012 from http://www.ptsd.va.gov/public/pages/cognitive_processing_therapy.asp

Department of Veterans Affairs. Clinical practice guideline for the management of Post-Traumatic Stress. Retrieved 9/112/2012 from http://www.healthquality.va.gov/ptsd/ptsd/_full.pdf

Department of Veterans Affairs. (2011). Suicide prevention. Washington, DC: Author. Retrieved from http://www.mentalhealth.va.gov/suicide_prevention/index.asp

Elbogen, E. B., Wagner, H. R., Fullert, S. R., Calhoun, P. S., & Kinneer, P. ; Mid-Atlantic Mental Illness Research, Education, and Clinical Center Workgroup, Beckham, JC. (2010). Correlates of anger and hostility in Iraq and Afghanistan war veterans. *American Journal of Psychiatry, 167* (9), 1051-1057.

Foa, E. B. & Kozak, J. J. (1986). Emotional processing of fear: Exposure to corrective information. *Psychological Bulletin, 99,* 20-35.

Grossman, D. A. (1995). *On killing: the psychological cost of learning to kill in war and society.* Boston: Little, Brown.

Guerra, V. S & Calhoun, P.S. (2010). Examining the relation between post-traumatic stress disorder and suicidal ideation in an OEF/OIF veteran sample. *Journal of Anxiety Disorder, 25* (1), 12-18.

Forgey, M. A., & Badger, L. (2006). Patterns of intimate partner violence among married women in the military: Type, level, directionality and consequences. *Journal of Family Violence, 21,* 369-380.

Hampton, T. (2007). Research, law address veteran's suicide. *Journal of the American Medical Association, 298 (*23), 27-32.

Hoge, C. W., Castro, C. A., Messner, D., McGurk, D., Cotting, D. I. & Koffman, R. L. (2004). Combat duty in Iraq and Afghanistan, mental health problems and barriers to care. *New England Journal of Medicine, 351 (1),* 13-23.

Jakupcak, M., Conybeare, D., Phelps, L., Hunt, S., Holmes, H. A., Felder, B., et al. (2007). Anger hostility, and aggression among Iraq and Afghanistan war veterans reporting PTSD and subthreshold PTSD. *Journal of Traumatic Stress, 20* (6), 945-954.

Johnson, W. B., Bacho, R., Heim, M. & Ralph, J. (2006). Multiple-role dilemmas for military mental health care providers. *Military Medicine, 171,* 4, 311-315.

Johnson, W. B., Grasso, I., & Maslowski, K. (2010). Conflicts between ethics and law for military mental health providers. *Military Medicine, 175,* 8, 548-553.

Kanel, K. (2014). *A Guide to Crisis Intervention, 5th Ed.* Pacific Grove, CA: Cengage.

Katz, L. S., Bloor, L. E., Cojucar, G. & Draper, T. (2007). Women who served in Iraq seeking mental health services: Relationships between Military Sexual Trauma, symptoms and readjustment. *Psychological Services, 4,* 4, 239-249.

Kennedy, K. (2010, August 9). Report links suicide spike to Army's focus on war. *Army Times,* p. 20.

Kitfield, J. (2012). The Enemy Within. *National Journal,* September 18, 2012. Retrieved from http://www.nationaljournal.com/magazine/the-military-s-rape-problem-20120913

Leaman, S., Rothbaum, B. O., Difede, J., Cukor, J., Cerardi, M., & Rizzo, A., (2013). Treating Combat-Related PTSD with virtual reality exposure therapy. In A. Rubin, E. L. Weiss, & J. E. Coll (Eds.) *Handbook of Military Social Work,* pp. 113-140, New Jersey: John Wiley & Sons

Lemaire, C. M. & Graham, D. P. (2011). Factors associated with suicidal ideation in OEF/OIF veterans. *Journal of Affective disorders, 130,* 231-238.

Loewenberg, F. M. & Dolgoff, R. (1992). *Ethical decisions for social work practice (4ᵗʰ ed.).* Itasca, IL: Peacock.

McDevitt-Murphy, M. E., Williams, J. L., Bracken, K.L., Fields, J. A., Monahan, C. J., & Murphy, J. G. (2010). PTSD symptoms, hazardous drinking, and health functioning among U.S. OEF and OIF veterans presenting to primary care. *Journal of Traumatic Stress, 23*, 1, 108-111.

McFarland, B. H., Kaplan, M. S. & Huguet, N. (2010). Self-inflicted deaths among women in the U.S. military service: A hidden epidemic? *Psychiatric Services, 61,* 12, 1177.

Mental Health Advisory Team V (MHAT –V). (2008). MHAT V. Operation Iraqi Freedom 06-08: Iraq. Operation enduring freedom 8: Afghanistan. Retrieved from http://www.armymedicine.army.mil/reports/mhat/mhat_v/mhat-v.cfm

Miliken, C. S., Auchterlonie, J. L., & Hoge, C. W. (2007). Longitudinal assessment of mental health problems among active and reserve component soldiers returning from the Iraq war. Journal of the American Medical Association, 298, 2141-2148.

Moore, B. A., & Kennedy, D. H. (2011). *Wheels down: Adjusting to life after deployment.* Washington, D. C. : APA Lifetools.

National Survey on Drug Use and Helath. (2008, November 6). Major depressive episode and treatment for depression among veterans aged 21-39. Retrieved from http://www.samhsa.gov/2k8/veteransDepressed/veteransDepressed.html.

Philipps, D. (2010). *Lethal warriors: When the new band of brothers came home.* New York, NY: Palgrave Macmillan.

Pierce, P. E. (2006). The role of women in the military. In T. W. Britt, A. B. Adler & C. A. Castro (Eds.). *Military Life: The psychology of serving in peace and combat* (pp. 97-118). Westport, CT: Greenwood.

Pryce, J. G., Pryce, D. H., & Shackelford, K. K. (2012). *The Costs of Courage Combat Stress, Warriors, and Family Survival.* Chicago, IL; Lyceum Books, Inc.

Rizzo, A. A., Reger, G., Gahm, G., Difede, J., & Rothbaum, B. O. (2009). Virtual reality exposure therapy for combat related PTSD. In P. Shiromani, T. Keane, & J. LeDoux (Eds.), *Post-traumatic stress disorder: Basic science and clinical practice* (pp. 375-399. New York, NY: Humana Press.

Schading, B. (2007). *A civilian's guide to the U.S. military: A comprehensive reference to the customs, language and structure of the armed forces.* Cincinnati, OH: Writer's Digest Books.

Selby, E. A., Anestis, M. D., Bender, T. W., Riberio, J. D., Nock, M. K., Rudd, M.D. et al. (2010). Overcoming fear of lethal injury: Evaluating suicidal behavior in the military through the lens of the interpersonal-psychological theory of suicide. *Clinical Psychology Review, 30,* 298-307.

Shay, J. (2009). The trials of homecoming: Odysseus returns from Iraq/Afghanistan. *Smith College Studies in Social Work, 79,* 286-298.

Shapiro, F., & Forrest, M. S. (1997). *EMDR.* New York: Basic Books.

Taber, K. & Hurley, R. (2009). PTSD and combat-related injuries: Functional neuroanatomy. *Journal of Neuropsychiatry and Clinical Neurosciences, 21,* iv-4.

Taft, C. T., Street, A. E., Marshall, A. D., Dowdall, D. J., & Riggs, D. S. (2007). Posttraumatic stress disorder, anger, and partner abuse among Vietnam combat veterans. Journal of Family Psychology, 21, 270-277.

Tarabay, J. (2010). Suicide rivals the battlefield in toll on U.S. military. Retrieved from http://www.npr.org/templates/story/story.php?storyId=127860466.

Tanielian, T., & Jaycox, L. (Eds.). (2008). *Invisible wounds of war: Psychological and cognitive injuries, their consequences and services to assist recovery.* Santa Monica, CA: RAND Corporation.

Teten, A. L., Miller, L. A., Stanford, M. S., Petersen, N. J., Bailey, S. D., Collins, R. L., et al. (2010). Characterizing aggression and its association to anger and hostility among male veterans with post traumatic stress disorder. *Military Medicine, 175* (6), 405-410.

Trego, L. L. (2007). Military women's menstrual experiences and interest in menstrual suppression during deployment. *Association of Women's health, Obstetric and Neonatal Nurses,* 342-347.

U.S. Department of Defense Task Force on Mental Health. (2007). An achievable vision: Report of the Department of Defense Task Force on Mental Health. Falls Church, VA: Defense Health Board.

U. S. Department of Veterans Affairs. (2011). New services for family caregivers of post-9/11 veterans. Retrieved from http://www.caregiver.va.gov/support_benefit.asp.

Veterans Health Administration. (2012). Aging veterans and posttraumatic stress symptom. Retrieved 12/11/2013) from http://www.ptsd.va.gov/public/pages/ptsd-older-vets.asp.

VHA Office of Public Health and Environmental Hazards. (2010). Analysis of VHA health care utilization among Operation Enduring Freedom (OEF) and Oeprpation Iraqi Freedom (OIF). Veterans, cumulative from 1st quarter FY 2002 through 4th quarter FY 2009. Retrieved from http://www.acatoday.org/ppt/4th QtrY090EF_OIF_HCU.ppt

Weiss, E. L., & DeBraber, T. (2013). Women in the Military. Found in the *Handbook of Military Social Work,* Edited by Rubin, A., Weiss, E. L. & Coll, J. E. John New Jersey: Wiley & Sons, Inc. p. 37-49.

Wolpe, J. (1973). *The practice of behavior therapy, 2nd ed.* New York, New York: Pergamon Press Inc.

Yarvis, J. S. & Schiess, L. (2008). Subthreshold PTSD as a predictor of depression, alcohol use, and health problems in soldiers. *Journal of Workplace Behavioral Health, 23,* 4.

Zwerdling D. (2009, July 21). Soldiers say Army ignores, punishes mental anguish. National Public Radio. Retrieved from http://www.npr.org/templates/story/story.php?storyld=6576505.

NOTES

NOTES

NOTES

NOTES

NOTES

NOTES

NOTES